PENGUIN TWENTIETH-CENTURY CLASSICS

LIFT EVERY VOICE AND SING

James Weldon Johnson was born in Jacksonville, Florida, in 1871. Among the first to break through the barriers segregating his race, he was educated at Atlanta University and at Columbia and was the first black admitted to the Florida bar. He was also, for a time, a songwriter in New York, American consul in Venezuela and Nicaragua, executive secretary of the NAACP, and professor of creative literature at Fisk University—experiences recorded in his autobiography, *Along This Way*. His other books include *The Autobiography of an Ex-Colored Man*, *Black Manhattan*, and *God's Trombones: Seven Negro Sermons in Verse*. In addition to his won writing, Johnson was the editor of pioneering anthologies of black American poetry and spirituals. He died in 1938.

LIFT EVERY VOICE
AND SING

SELECTED POEMS

BY

JAMES WELDON JOHNSON

WITH A PREFACE BY
SONDRA KATHRYN WILSON

PENGUIN BOOKS

PENGUIN BOOKS
Published by the Penguin Group
Penguin Putnam Inc., 375 Hudson Street,
New York, New York 10014, U.S.A.
Penguin Books Ltd, 27 Wrights Lane,
London W8 5TZ, England
Penguin Books Australia Ltd,
Ringwood, Victoria, Australia
Penguin Books Canada Ltd, 10 Alcorn Avenue,
Toronto, Ontario, Canada M4V 3B2
Penguin Books (N.Z.) Ltd, 182–190 Wairau Road,
Auckland 10, New Zealand

Penguin Books Ltd, Registered Offices:
Harmondsworth, Middlesex, England

First published in the United States of America under the title
St. Peter Relates an Incident: Selected Poems by The Viking Press, Inc., 1935
Published with a preface by Sondra Kathryn Wilson in Penguin Books 1993
This edition with the title *Lift Every Voice and Sing*
published in Penguin Books 2000

1   3   5   7   9   10   8   6   4   2

ISBN 0 14 11.8387 X
(CIP data available)

Printed in the United States of America
Set in Janson

TO G. N. J.

PREFACE

If I had to define the feelings, ideas, and thoughts of James Weldon Johnson as a litterateur and poet in one word, it would be "universality." "Universality" because he used his brilliance and blackness to reveal some of the most obscure expressions of black culture through literature. He elevated those aspects of the Black Experience into American life and world culture. Johnson declared that it is through the production and interpretation of a race's literature and other creative expressions that a people can begin to break down the stereotypical conceptions that are so inherent in universal thought.

In his own literary canon, Johnson demonstrates that no one race can lay claim to universality. For example, in "O Black and Unknown Bards," a poem included in this collection, Johnson's prototypes, the faceless and nameless slaves, come to life as universals. In this poem and in much of his other literary writings, we see Johnson using the particular to explain the universal. And he simultaneously uses the universal to explain the particular. "O Black and Unknown Bards" touches upon the unique creative genius of a people while enslaved and how that genius manifested itself in the form of the "Negro" spirituals. Out of the hearts and souls of the slaves came such melodies as "Steal Away Jesus," "Singing with a Sword in My Hand," "Rule Death in His Arms," and "The Blood Came Twinklin' Down." Johnson notes that the imagination of the "Black and Unknown Bards" was sparked by the vivid biblical stories they heard. They fused these stories with the suffering and pathos of their own lives in musical form. These creators didn't record their creations themselves, but Johnson became an instrument for reproducing the black racial spirit in art form.

Johnson's success as a poet is anchored in the oral traditions of his people. He realized that it was only out of these sources that the power—sometimes mythic, sometimes symbolic—came to withstand racism. The African-American Tradition as conceived by Johnson was dependent on its ability to relate itself to the human situation unique to oppressed people in general and black people in particular. To the extent that Johnson did this is the extent to which he can be said to be really successful.

In the poems included in *Lift Every Voice and Sing*, we see him integrating the feelings and forces of black life, offering poems with general themes. The poems by Johnson presented in this volume can be viewed within two distinct contexts. The first consists of poems built upon racial themes but with universal appeal: mainly protest poems and poems in dialect. The second is comprised of themes expressing universal sentiments.

Johnson's protest poems represent the union of his political experience and his creative talent. As an antilynching crusader in the early civil rights movement, Johnson wrote the poem "Brothers" in 1916. Deft in feeling, this poem expresses a dialogue between the mob and the black victim that has been going on for three centuries in America. The theme in Johnson's protest poems is his challenge to black Americans that they make this country as much their land as it is the land of white citizens. As he writes in the poem "Fifty Years," "This land is ours by right of birth. This land is ours by right of toil."

He began writing dialect poems a few years before the onset of the twentieth century but discarded the form about 1910. Initially reluctant to include his dialect poems in this volume, he quickly realized that the attempt to exclude them from American literature would cause both a racial and national loss. These poems are evocative of the "color" and "flavor" of black life in the backwoods, the cottonfield, and the canebrake. His literary mentor, Brander Matthews, described Johnsons's dialect poems as "racy of the soil, pungent in flavor, swinging in rhythm, and adroit in rhyme."

The poetry of the first tradition manifests protest, challenge, and hope. In the poems of the second tradition, however, Johnson's artistry is not imbued by the polemical aspects of the race problem. The sentiments expressed in this selection are common to all humankind. Matthews characterized these poems, including "Mother, Farewell!," "My City," and "Girl of Fifteen," as "delicate in workmanship [and] fragrant with sentiment."

Johnson included his most famous poem, "Lift Every Voice and Sing," in this volume. Written in 1900 and set to music by his brother J. Rosamond Johnson, the song was originally called the Negro National Hymn. By the 1920s African-Americans had made the song their national anthem. "Lift Every Voice and Sing" embodies the history, hopes, and aspirations of African-Americans in this nation, "Nothing that I have done has paid me back so fully in satisfaction as being part creator of this song," Johnson wrote.

It was James Weldon Johnson who revealed to America and to the world the creative genius of obscure figures like the "unlettered" black bards and the old-time black preachers in his *God's Trombones: Seven Negro Sermons in Verse*. Through his own writings, he helped to build the African-American tradition in American literature based on the developing black ethos. *Lift Every Voice and Sing* is his gift to us of that truly rich tradition.

Sondra Kathryn Wilson

Contents

FOREWORD

"Saint Peter Relates an Incident" was originally printed in 1930, in an edition of 200 copies for private distribution. In the summer of that year the author was busy on the manuscript of a book. He read one morning in the newspaper that the United States government was sending a contingent of gold-star mothers to France to visit the graves of their soldier sons buried there; and that the Negro gold-star mothers would not be allowed to sail on the same ship with the white gold-star mothers, but would be sent over on a second and second-class vessel. He threw aside the manuscript on which he was working and did not take it up again until he had finished the poem, "Saint Peter Relates an Incident of the Resurrection Day."

The dedicatory lines in the original edition were:

> *Written while meditating upon heaven and hell and democracy and war and America and the Negro Gold Star Mothers.*

The bulk of the poems in this volume have been selected from *Fifty Years and Other Poems*, the author's first book of verse, now out of print. A small number are poems not heretofore published in book form.

Saint Peter
Relates an Incident
of the Resurrection Day

Saint Peter Relates an Incident
of the Resurrection Day

Eternities—now numbering six or seven—
Hung heavy on the hands of all in heaven.
Archangels tall and fair had reached the stage
Where they began to show some signs of age.

The faces of the flaming seraphim
Were slightly drawn, their eyes were slightly dim.
The cherubs, too, for now—oh, an infinite while
Had worn but a wistful shade of their dimpling smile.

The serried singers of the celestial choir
Disclosed a woeful want of pristine fire;
When they essayed to strike the glad refrain,
Their attack was weak, their tone revealed voice strain.

Their expression seemed to say, "We must! We must!"
        though
'Twas more than evident they lacked the gusto;
It could not be elsewise—that fact all can agree on—
Chanting the selfsame choral æon after æon.

Thus was it that Saint Peter at the gate
Began a brand new thing in heaven: to relate
Some reminiscences from heavenly history,
Which had till then been more or less a mystery.

So now and then, by turning back the pages,
Were whiled away some moments from the ages,
Was gained a respite from the monotony
That can't help settling on eternity.

Now, there had been a lapse of ages hoary,
And the angels clamored for another story.
"Tell us a tale, Saint Peter," they entreated;
And gathered close around where he was seated.

Saint Peter stroked his beard,
And "Yes," he said
By the twinkle in his eye
And the nodding of his head.

A moment brief he fumbled with his keys—
It seemed to help him call up memories—
Straightway there flashed across his mind the one
About the unknown soldier
Who came from Washington.

The hosts stood listening,
Breathlessly awake;
And thus Saint Peter spake:

'Twas Resurrection morn,
And Gabriel blew a blast upon his horn
That echoed through the arches high and vast
Of Time and Space—a long resounding blast

To wake the dead, dead for a million years;
A blast to reach and pierce their dust-stopped ears;
To quicken them, wherever they might be,
Deep in the earth or deeper in the sea.

A shudder shook the world, and gaping graves
Gave up their dead. Out from the parted waves
Came the prisoners of old ocean. The dead belonging
To every land and clime came thronging.

From the four corners of all the earth they drew,
Their faces radiant and their bodies new.
Creation pulsed and swayed beneath the tread
Of all the living, and all the risen dead.

Swift-winged heralds of heaven flew back and forth,
Out of the east, to the south, the west, the north,
Giving out quick commands, and yet benign,
Marshaling the swarming milliards into line.

The recording angel in words of thundering might,
At which the timid, doubting souls took fright,
Bade all to await the grand roll-call; to wit,
To see if in the Book their names were writ.

The multitudinous business of the day
Progressed, but naturally, not without delay.
Meanwhile, within the great American border
There was the issuance of a special order.

The word went forth, spoke by some grand panjandrum,
Perhaps, by some high potentate of Klandom,
That all the trusty patriotic mentors,
And duly qualified Hundred-Percenters

Should forthwith gather together upon the banks
Of the Potomac, there to form their ranks,
March to the tomb, by orders to be given,
And escort the unknown soldier up to heaven.

Compliantly they gathered from each region,
The G.A.R., the D.A.R., the Legion,
Veterans of wars—Mexican, Spanish, Haitian—
Trustees of the patriotism of the nation;

Key Men, Watchmen, shunning circumlocution,
The Sons of the This and That and of the Revolution;
Not to forget, there gathered every man
Of the Confederate Veterans and the Ku-Klux Klan.

The Grand Imperial Marshal gave the sign;
Column on column, the marchers fell in line;
Majestic as an army in review,
They swept up Washington's wide avenue.

Then, through the long line ran a sudden flurry,
The marchers in the rear began to hurry;
They feared unless the procession hastened on,
The unknown soldier might be risen and gone.

The fear was groundless; when they arrived, in fact,
They found the grave entirely intact.
(Resurrection plans were long, long past completing
Ere there was thought of re-enforced concreting.)

They heard a faint commotion in the tomb,
Like the stirring of a child within the womb;
At once they saw the plight, and set about
The job to dig the unknown soldier out.

They worked away, they labored with a will,
They toiled with pick, with crowbar, and with drill
To cleave a breach; nor did the soldier shirk;
Within his limits, he helped to push the work.

He, underneath the débris, heaved and hove
Up toward the opening which they cleaved and clove;
Through it, at last, his towering form loomed
    big and bigger—
"Great God Almighty! Look!" they cried,
    "he is a nigger!"

Surprise and consternation and dismay
Swept over the crowd; none knew just what to say
Or what to do. And all fell back aghast.
Silence—but only an instant did it last.

Bedlam: They clamored, they railed, some roared, some
    bleated;
All of them felt that somehow they'd been cheated.
The question rose: What to do with him, then?
The Klan was all for burying him again.

The scheme involved within the Klan's suggestion
Gave rise to a rather nice metaphysical question:
Could he be forced again through death's dark portal,
Since now his body and soul were both immortal?

Would he, forsooth, the curious-minded queried,
Even in concrete, re-entombed, stay buried?
In a moment more, midst the pile of broken stone,
The unknown soldier stood, and stood alone.

V

The day came to a close.
And heaven—hell too—was filled with them that rose.
I shut the pearly gate and turned the key;
For Time was now merged into Eternity.

I gave one last look over the jasper wall,
And afar descried a figure dark and tall:
The unknown soldier, dust-stained and begrimed,
Climbing his way to heaven, and singing as he climbed:
    Deep river, my home is over Jordan,
    Deep river, I want to cross over into camp-ground.

Climbing and singing—
    Deep river, my home is over Jordan,
    Deep river, I want to cross over into camp-ground.

Nearer and louder—
    Deep river, my home is over Jordan,
    Deep river, I want to cross over into camp-ground.

At the jasper wall—
    Deep river, my home is over Jordan,
    Deep river,
    Lord,
    I want to cross over into camp-ground.

I rushed to the gate and flung it wide,
Singing, he entered with a loose, long stride;
Singing and swinging up the golden street,
The music married to the tramping of his feet.

Tall, black soldier-angel marching alone,
Swinging up the golden street, saluting at the great white
  throne.
Singing, singing, singing, singing clear and strong.
Singing, singing, singing, till heaven took up the song:
  Deep river, my home is over Jordan,
  Deep river, I want to cross over into camp-ground.

The tale was done,
The angelic hosts dispersed,
   but not till after
There ran through heaven
Something that quivered
   'twixt tears and laughter.

Selected Poems

O Black and Unknown Bards

O black and unknown bards of long ago,
How came your lips to touch the sacred fire?
How, in your darkness, did you come to know
The power and beauty of the minstrel's lyre?
Who first from midst his bonds lifted his eyes?
Who first from out the still watch, lone and long,
Feeling the ancient faith of prophets rise
Within his dark-kept soul, burst into song?

Heart of what slave poured out such melody
As "Steal Away to Jesus"? On its strains
His spirit must have nightly floated free,
Though still about his hands he felt his chains.
Who heard great "Jordan roll"? Whose starward eye
Saw chariot "swing low"? And who was he
That breathed that comforting, melodic sigh,
"Nobody Knows de Trouble I See"?

What merely living clod, what captive thing,
Could up toward God through all its darkness grope,
And find within its deadened heart to sing
These songs of sorrow, love, and faith, and hope?
How did it catch that subtle undertone,
That note in music heard not with the ears?
How sound the elusive reed so seldom blown,
Which stirs the soul or melts the heart to tears?

Not that great German master in his dream
Of harmonies that thundered amongst the stars
At the creation, ever heard a theme
Nobler than "Go Down, Moses." Mark its bars,
How like a mighty trumpet-call they stir
The blood. Such are the notes that men have sung
Going to valorous deeds; such tones there were
That helped make history when Time was young.

There is a wide, wide wonder in it all,
That from degraded rest and servile toil
The fiery spirit of the seer should call
These simple children of the sun and soil.
O black slave singers, gone, forgot, unfamed,
You—you alone, of all the long, long line
Of those who've sung untaught, unknown, unnamed,
Have stretched out upward, seeking the divine.

You sang not deeds of heroes or of kings;
No chant of bloody war, no exulting pæan
Of arms-won triumphs; but your humble strings
You touched in chord with music empyrean.
You sang far better than you knew; the songs
That for your listeners' hungry hearts sufficed
Still live—but more than this to you belongs:
You sang a race from wood and stone to Christ.

Brothers—American Drama

(THE MOB SPEAKS:)
  See! There he stands; not brave, but with an air
  Of sullen stupor. Mark him well! Is he
  Not more like brute than man? Look in his eye!
  No light is there; none, save the glint that shines
  In the now glaring, and now shifting orbs
  Of some wild animal caught in the hunter's trap.

  How came this beast in human shape and form?
  Speak man!—We call you man because you wear
  His shape—How are you thus? Are you not from
  That docile, child-like, tender-hearted race
  Which we have known three centuries? Not from
  That more than faithful race which through three wars
  Fed our dear wives and nursed our helpless babes
  Without a single breach of trust? Speak out!

(THE VICTIM SPEAKS:)
  I am, and am not.

(THE MOB SPEAKS AGAIN:)
                    Then who, why are you?

(THE VICTIM SPEAKS AGAIN:)
  I am a thing not new, I am as old
  As human nature. I am that which lurks,
  Ready to spring whenever a bar is loosed;

The ancient trait which fights incessantly
Against restraint, balks at the upward climb;
The weight forever seeking to obey
The law of downward pull—and I am more:
The bitter fruit am I of planted seed;
The resultant, the inevitable end
Of evil forces and the powers of wrong.

Lessons in degradation, taught and learned,
The memories of cruel sights and deeds,
The pent-up bitterness, the unspent hate
Filtered through fifteen generations have
Sprung up and found in me sporadic life.
In me the muttered curse of dying men,
On me the stain of conquered women, and
Consuming me the fearful fires of lust,
Lit long ago, by other hands than mine.
In me the down-crushed spirit, the hurled-back
        prayers
Of wretches now long dead—their dire bequests.
In me the echo of the stifled cry
Of children for their bartered mothers' breasts.

I claim no race, no race claims me; I am
No more than human dregs; degenerate;
The monstrous offspring of the monster, Sin;
I am—just what I am. . . . The race that fed
Your wives and nursed your babes would do the same
Today. But I——

(THE MOB CONCLUDES:)
                    Enough, the brute must die!
Quick! Chain him to that oak! It will resist
The fire much longer than this slender pine.
Now bring the fuel! Pile it round him! Wait!
Pile not so fast or high! or we shall lose
The agony and terror in his face.
And now the torch! Good fuel that! the flames
Already leap head-high. Ha! hear that shriek!
And there's another! wilder than the first.
Fetch water! Water! Pour a little on
The fire, lest it should burn too fast. Hold so!
Now let it slowly blaze again. See there!
He squirms! He groans! His eyes bulge wildly out,
Searching around in vain appeal for help!
Another shriek, the last! Watch how the flesh
Grows crisp and hangs till, turned to ash, it sifts
Down through the coils of chain that hold erect
The ghastly frame against the bark-scorched tree.

Stop! to each man no more than one man's share.
You take that bone, and you this tooth; the chain,
Let us divide its links; this skull, of course,
In fair division, to the leader comes.

And now his fiendish crime has been avenged;
Let us back to our wives and children—say,
What did he mean by those last muttered words,
"Brothers in spirit, brothers in deed are we"?

O Southland!

O Southland! O Southland!
  Have you not heard the call,
The trumpet blown, the word made known
  To the nations, one and all?
The watchword, the hope-word,
  Salvation's present plan?
A gospel new, for all—for you:
  Man shall be saved by man.

O Southland! O Southland!
  Do you not hear today
The mighty beat of onward feet,
  And know you not their way?
'Tis forward, 'tis upward,
  On to the fair white arch
Of Freedom's dome, and there is room
  For each man who would march.

O Southland, fair Southland!
  Then why do you still cling
To an idle age and a musty page,
  To a dead and useless thing?
'Tis springtime! 'Tis work-time!
  The world is young again!
And God's above, and God is love,
  And men are only men.

We to America

How would you have us, as we are—
Or sinking 'neath the load we bear?
Our eyes fixed forward on a star—
Or gazing empty at despair?

Rising or falling? Men or things?
With dragging pace or footsteps fleet?
Strong, willing sinews in your wings?
Or tightening chains about your feet?

Mother Night

Eternities before the first-born day,
    Or ere the first sun fledged his wings of flame,
    Calm Night, the everlasting and the same,
    A brooding mother over chaos lay.
And whirling suns shall blaze and then decay,
    Shall run their fiery courses and then claim
    The haven of the darkness whence they came;
    Back to Nirvanic peace shall grope their way.

So when my feeble sun of life burns out,
    And sounded is the hour for my long sleep,
    I shall, full weary of the feverish light,
Welcome the darkness without fear or doubt,
    And heavy-lidded, I shall softly creep
    Into the quiet bosom of the Night.

The Young Warrior

Mother, shed no mournful tears,
But gird me on my sword;
And give no utterance to thy fears,
But bless me with thy word.

The lines are drawn! The fight is on!
A cause is to be won!
Mother, look not so paled and wan;
Give Godspeed to thy son.

Now let thine eyes my way pursue
Where'er my footsteps fare;
And when they lead beyond thy view,
Send after me a prayer.

But pray not to defend from harm,
Nor danger to dispel;
Pray, rather, that with steadfast arm
I fight the battle well.

Pray, mother of mine, that I always keep
My heart and purpose strong,
My sword unsullied and ready to leap
Unsheathed against the wrong.

The White Witch

O brothers mine, take care! Take care!
The great white witch rides out tonight,
Trust not your prowess nor your strength;
Your only safety lies in flight;
For in her glance there is a snare,
And in her smile there is a blight.

The great white witch you have not seen?
Then, younger brothers mine, forsooth,
Like nursery children you have looked
For ancient hag and snaggle-tooth;
But no, not so; the witch appears
In all the glowing charms of youth.

Her lips are like carnations red,
Her face like new-born lilies fair,
Her eyes like ocean waters blue,
She moves with subtle grace and air,
And all about her head there floats
The golden glory of her hair.

But though she always thus appears
In form of youth and mood of mirth,
Unnumbered centuries are hers,
The infant planets saw her birth;
The child of throbbing Life is she,
Twin sister to the greedy earth.

And back behind those smiling lips,
And down within those laughing eyes,
And underneath the soft caress
Of hand and voice and purring sighs,
The shadow of the panther lurks,
The spirit of the vampire lies.

For I have seen the great white witch,
And she has led me to her lair,
And I have kissed her red, red lips
And cruel face so white and fair;
Around me she has twined her arms,
And bound me with her yellow hair.

I felt those red lips burn and sear
My body like a living coal;
Obeyed the power of those eyes
As the needle trembles to the pole;
And did not care although I felt
The strength go ebbing from my soul.

Oh! she has seen your strong young limbs,
And heard your laughter loud and gay,
And in your voices she has caught
The echo of a far-off day,
When man was closer to the earth;
And she has marked you for her prey.

She feels the old Antæan strength
In you, the great dynamic beat
Of primal passions, and she sees
In you the last besieged retreat
Of love relentless, lusty, fierce,
Love pain-ecstatic, cruel-sweet.

O, brothers mine, take care! Take care!
The great white witch rides out tonight.
O, younger brothers mine, beware!
Look not upon her beauty bright;
For in her glance there is a snare,
And in her smile there is a blight.

My City

When I come down to sleep death's endless night,
The threshold of the unknown dark to cross,
What to me then will be the keenest loss,
When this bright world blurs on my fading sight?
Will it be that no more I shall see the trees
Or smell the flowers or hear the singing birds
Or watch the flashing streams or patient herds?
No. I am sure it will be none of these.

But, ah! Manhattan's sights and sounds, her smells,
Her crowds, her throbbing force, the thrill that comes
From being of her a part, her subtle spells,
Her shining towers, her avenues, her slums—
O God! the stark, unutterable pity,
To be dead, and never again behold my city.

The Glory of the Day Was in Her Face

The glory of the day was in her face,
The beauty of the night was in her eyes.
And over all her loveliness, the grace
Of morning blushing in the early skies.

And in her voice, the calling of the dove;
Like music of a sweet, melodious part.
And in her smile, the breaking light of love;
And all the gentle virtues in her heart.

And now the glorious day, the beauteous night,
The birds that signal to their mates at dawn,
To my dull ears, to my tear-blinded sight
Are one with all the dead, since she is gone.

Life

Out of the infinite sea of eternity
To climb, and for an instant stand
Upon an island speck of time.

From the impassible peace of the darkness
To wake, and blink at the garish light
Through one short space of fretfulness.

The Black Mammy

O whitened head entwined in turban gay,
O kind black face, O crude, but tender hand,
O foster-mother in whose arms there lay
The race whose sons are masters of the land!
It was thine arms that sheltered in their fold,
It was thine eyes that followed through the length
Of infant days these sons. In times of old
It was thy breast that nourished them to strength.

So often hast thou to thy bosom pressed
The golden head, the face and brow of snow;
So often has it 'gainst thy broad, dark breast
Lain, set off like a quickened cameo.
Thou simple soul, as cuddling down that babe
With thy sweet croon, so plaintive and so wild,
Came ne'er the thought to thee, swift like a stab,
That it some day might crush thy own black child?

Fragment

The hand of Fate cannot be stayed,
The course of Fate cannot be steered,
By all the gods that man has made,
Nor all the devils he has feared,
Not by the prayers that might be prayed
In all the temples he has reared.

See! In your very midst there dwell
Ten thousand thousand blacks, a wedge
Forged in the furnaces of hell,
And sharpened to a cruel edge
By wrong and by injustice fell,
And driven by hatred as a sledge.

A wedge so slender at the start—
Just twenty slaves in shackles bound—
And yet which split the land apart
With shrieks of war and battle sound,
Which pierced the nation's very heart,
And still lies cankering in the wound.

Not all the glory of your pride,
Preserved in story and in song,
Can from the judging future hide,
Through all the coming ages long,
That though you bravely fought and died,
You fought and died for what was wrong.

'Tis fixed—for them that violate
The eternal laws, naught shall avail
Till they their error expiate;
Nor shall their unborn children fail
To pay the full required weight
Into God's great, unerring scale.

Think not repentance can redeem,
That sin his wages can withdraw;
No, think as well to change the scheme
Of worlds that move in reverent awe;
Forgiveness is an idle dream,
God is not love, no, God is law.

Mother, Farewell!

(From the Spanish of Plácido. Written in the chapel of the Hospital de Santa Cristina on the night before his execution.) *

If the unfortunate fate engulfing me,
The ending of my history of grief,
The closing of my span of years so brief,
Mother, should wake a single pang in thee,
Weep not. No saddening thought to me devote;
I calmly go to a death that is glory-filled;
My lyre before it is forever stilled
Breathes out to thee its last and dying note.

A note scarce more than a burden-easing sigh,
Tender and sacred, innocent, sincere,
Spontaneous and instinctive as the cry
I gave at birth. And now the hour is here—
O God, thy mantle of mercy over my sins!
Mother, farewell! The pilgrimage begins.

* See page 105.

Girl of Fifteen

Girl of fifteen,
I see you each morning from my window
As you pass on your way to school.
I do more than see, I watch you.
I furtively draw the curtain aside.
And my heart leaps through my eyes
And follows you down the street;
Leaving me behind, half-hid
And wholly ashamed.

What holds me back,
Half-hid behind the curtains and wholly ashamed,
But my forty years beyond your fifteen?

Girl of fifteen, as you pass
There passes, too, a lightning flash of time
In which you lift those forty summers off my head,
And take those forty winters out of my heart.

The Suicide

For fifty years,
Cruel, insatiable old World,
You have punched me over the heart
Till you made me cough blood.
The few paltry things I gathered
You snatched out of my hands.
You have knocked the cup from my thirsty lips.
You have laughed at my hunger of body and soul.

You look at me now and think,
"He is still strong,
There ought to be twenty more years of good punching
        there.
At the end of that time he will be old and broken,
Not able to strike back,
But cringing and crying for leave
To live a little longer."

Those twenty, pitiful, extra years
Would please you more than the fifty past,
Would they not, old World?
Well, I hold them up before your greedy eyes,
And snatch them away as I laugh in your face.
Ha——

Down by the Carib Sea

I

SUNRISE IN THE TROPICS

Sol, Sol, mighty lord of the tropic zone,
Here I wait with the trembling stars
To see thee once more take thy throne.

There the patient palm tree watching
Waits to say "Good morn" to thee,
And a throb of expectation
Pulses through the earth and me.

Now over nature falls a hush,
Look! the east is all a-blush;
And a growing crimson crest
Dims the late stars in the west;
Now, a wave of vivid light
Sweeps away the shimmering night.
See! the miracle is done!
Once more behold, the Sun!

II

LOS CIGARRILLOS

This is the land of the dark-eyed *gente*,
Of the *dolce far niente*,

Where we dream away
Both the night and day.
At night-time in sleep our dreams we invoke,
Our dreams come by day through the redolent smoke,
As it lazily curls,
And slowly unfurls
From our lips,
And the tips
Of our fragrant *cigarrillos*.
For life in the tropics is only a joke,
So we pass it in dreams, and we pass it in smoke,
Smoke——smoke——smoke.

Tropical constitutions
Call for occasional revolutions,
But after that's through,
Why there's nothing to do
But smoke——smoke;

For life in the tropics is only a joke,
So we pass it in dreams, and we pass it in smoke,
Smoke——smoke——smoke.

I I I

TEESTAY*

Of tropic sensations, the worst
Is, *sin duda*, the tropical thirst.

* *Tiste* is a popular drink in Nicaragua.

When it starts in your throat and constantly grows,
Till you feel that it reaches down to your toes,
When your mouth tastes like fur
And your tongue turns to dust,
There's but one thing to do,
And do it you must,
Drink *teestay*.

Teestay, a drink with a history,
A delicious, delectable mystery,
"*Cinco centavos el vaso, señor,*
If you take one, you will surely want more."

Teestay, teestay,
The national drink on a feast day;
How it coolingly tickles,
As downward it trickles,
Teestay, teestay.

And you wish, as you take it down at a quaff,
That your neck was constructed à la giraffe.
Teestay, teestay.

I V

THE LOTTERY GIRL

"Lottery, lottery,
Take a chance at the lottery?
Take a ticket,
Or, better, take two;

Who knows what the future
May hold for you?
Lottery, lottery,
Take a chance at the lottery?"

Oh, limpid-eyed girl,
I would take every chance,
If only the prize
Were a love-flashing glance
From your fathomless eyes.

"Lottery, lottery,
Try your luck at the lottery?
Consider the size
Of the capital prize,
And take tickets
For the lottery.
Tickets, *señor?* Tickets, *señor?*
Take a chance at the lottery?"

Oh, crimson-lipped girl,
With the magical smile,
I would count that the gamble
Were well worth the while,
Not a chance would I miss,
If only the prize
Were a honey-bee kiss
Gathered in sips
From those full-ripened lips,
And a love-flashing glance
From your eyes.

V

THE DANCING GIRL

Do you know what it is to dance?
Perhaps, you do know, in a fashion;
But by dancing I mean,
Not what's generally seen,
But dancing of fire and passion,
Of fire and delirious passion.

With a dusky-haired *señorita*,
Her dark, misty eyes near your own,
And her scarlet-red mouth,
Like a rose of the south,
The reddest that ever was grown,
So close that you catch
Her quick-panting breath
As across your own face it is blown,
With a sigh, and a moan.

Ah! that is dancing,
As here by the Carib it's known.

Now, whirling and twirling
Like furies we go;
Now, soft and caressing
And sinuously slow;
With an undulating motion,
Like waves on a breeze-kissed ocean—
And the scarlet-red mouth
Is nearer your own,

And the dark, misty eyes
Still softer have grown.

Ah! that is dancing, that is dancing,
As here by the Carib it's known.

V I

SUNSET IN THE TROPICS

A silver flash from the sinking sun,
Then a shot of crimson across the sky
That, bursting, lets a thousand colors fly
And riot among the clouds; they run,
Deepening in purple, flaming in gold,
Changing, and opening fold after fold,
Then fading through all of the tints of the rose into gray,
Till, taking quick fright at the coming night,
They rush out down the west,
In hurried quest
Of the fleeing day.

Now above, where the tardiest color flares a moment yet,
One point of light, now two, now three are set
To form the starry stairs—
And, in her firefly crown,
Queen Night, on velvet slippered feet, comes softly
down.

Deep in the Quiet Wood

Are you bowed down in heart?
Do you but hear the clashing discords and the din of life?
Then come away, come to the peaceful wood.
Here bathe your soul in silence. Listen! Now,
From out the palpitating solitude
Do you not catch, yet faint, elusive strains?
They are above, around, within you, everywhere.
Silently listen! Clear, and still more clear, they come.
They bubble up in rippling notes, and swell in singing
     tones.
Now let your soul run the whole gamut of the wondrous
     scale
Until, responsive to the tonic chord,
It touches the diapason of God's grand cathedral organ,
Filling earth for you with heavenly peace
And holy harmonies.

Prayer at Sunrise

O mighty, powerful, dark-dispelling sun,
Now thou art risen, and thy day begun.
How shrink the shrouding mists before thy face,
As up thou spring'st to thy diurnal race!
How darkness chases darkness to the west,
As shades of light on light rise radiant from thy crest!
For thee, great source of strength, emblem of might,
In hours of darkest gloom there is no night.
Thou shinest on though clouds hide thee from sight,
And through each break thou sendest down thy light.

O greater Maker of this Thy great sun,
Give me the strength this one day's race to run;
Fill me with light, fill me with sun-like strength;
Fill me with joy to rob the day its length.
Light from within, light that will outward shine,
Strength to make strong some weaker heart than mine,
Joy to make glad each soul that feels its touch;
Great Father of the sun, I ask this much.

Her Eyes Twin Pools

Her eyes, twin pools of mystic light,
The blend of star-sheen and black night;
O'er which, to sound their glamouring haze,
A man might bend, and vainly gaze.

Her eyes, twin pools so dark and deep,
In which life's ancient mysteries sleep;
Wherein, to seek the quested goal,
A man might plunge, and lose his soul.

Vashti

I sometimes take you in my dreams to a far-off land I
    used to know,
Back in the ages long ago; a land of palms and languid
    streams.

A land, by night, of jeweled skies, by day, of shores that
    glistened bright,
Within whose arms, outstretched and white, a sapphire
    sea lay crescent-wise.

Where twilight fell like silver floss, where rose the
    golden moon half-hid
Behind a shadowy pyramid; a land beneath the Southern
    Cross.

And there the days dreamed in their flight, each one a
    poem chanted through,
Which at its close was merged into the muted music of
    the night.

And you were a princess in those days. And I—I was your
    serving lad.
But who ever served with heart so glad, or lived so for
    a word of praise?

And if that word you chanced to speak, how all my
    senses swayed and reeled,

Till low beside your feet I kneeled, with happiness
    o'erwrought and weak.

If, when your golden cup I bore, you deigned to lower
    your eyes to mine,
Eyes cold, yet fervid, like the wine, I knew not how to
    wish for more.

I trembled at the thought to dare to gaze upon, to
    scrutinize
The deep-sea mystery of your eyes, the sun-lit splendor
    of your hair.

To let my timid glances rest upon you long enough to
    note
How fair and slender was your throat, how white the
    promise of your breast.

But though I did not dare to chance a lingering look, an
    open gaze
Upon your beauty's blinding rays, I ventured many a
    stolen glance.

I fancy, too (but could not state what trick of mind the
    fancy caused),
At times your eyes upon me paused, and marked my
    figure lithe and straight.

Once when my eyes met yours it seemed that in your
    cheek, despite your pride,

A flush arose and swiftly died; or was it something that
    I dreamed?

Within your radiance like the star of morning, there I
    stood and served,
Close by, unheeded, unobserved. You were so near, and,
    yet, so far.

Ah! just to stretch my hand and touch the musky sandals
    on your feet!—
My breaking heart! of rapture sweet it never could have
    held so much.

Oh, beauty-haunted memory! Your face so proud, your
    eyes so calm,
Your body like a slim young palm, and sinuous as a
    willow tree.

Caught up beneath your slender arms, and girdled round
    your supple waist,
A robe of curious silk that graced, but only scarce
    concealed your charms.

A golden band about your head, a crimson jewel at your
    throat
Which, when the sunlight on it smote, turned to a living
    heart and bled.

But oh, that mystic bleeding stone, that work of nature's
    magic art,

Which mimicked so a wounded heart, could never bleed
    as did my own!

   .   .   .   .

Now after ages long and sad, in this stern land we meet
    anew;
No more a princess proud are you, and I—I am no serving
    lad.

And, yet, dividing us, I meet a wider gulf than that which
    stood
Between a princess of the blood and him who served
    low at her feet.

If I Were Paris

Not for me the budding girl
Or the maiden in full bloom,
Sure of beauty and of charm,
Careless of the distant doom,
Laughing in the face of years
That stretch out so long and far,
Mindful of the things to be,
Heedless of the things that are;

But the woman sweetly ripe,
Under the autumn of her skies;
Thin lines of care about her mouth,
And utterless longings in her eyes.

Ghosts of the Old Year

The snow has ceased its fluttering flight,
The wind sunk to a whisper light,
An ominous stillness fills the night,
   A pause—a hush.
At last, a sound that breaks the spell,
Loud, clanging mouthings of a bell,
That through the silence peal and swell,
   And roll, and rush.

What does this brazen tongue declare,
That falling on the midnight air
Brings to my heart a sense of care
   Akin to fright?
'Tis telling that the year is dead,
The New Year come, the Old Year fled,
Another leaf before me spread
   On which to write.

It tells of deeds that were not done,
It tells of races never run,
Of victories that were not won,
   Barriers unleaped.
It tells of many a squandered day,
Of slighted gems and treasured clay,
Of precious stores not laid away,
   Of fields unreaped.

And so the years go swiftly by,
Each, coming, brings ambitions high,
And each, departing, leaves a sigh
  Linked to the past.
Large resolutions, little deeds;
Thus, filled with aims unreached, life speeds,
Until the blotted record reads,
  "Failure!" at last.

Beauty Never Old

When buffeted and beaten by life's storms,
When by the bitterness of life oppressed,
I need no surer haven than your arms,
I want no happier shelter than your breast.

When over my way there falls the sudden blight
Of sunless days and nights of starless skies,
Enough for me the ever-steadfast light
I know is always shining in your eyes.

The world, for me,
And all the world can hold
Is circled by your arms;
For me there lies
Within the lighted shadows of your eyes
The only beauty that is never old.

Blessed Sleep

Blessed sleep, kindest minister to man,
Sure and silent distiller of the balm of rest,
Having alone the power, when naught else can,
To soothe the torn and sorrow-ridden breast.
When bleeding hearts no comforter can find,
When burdened souls droop under weight of woe,
When thought is torture to the troubled mind,
When grief-relieving tears refuse to flow,
Respite but comes on sleep's faint-beating wings;
From them oblivion's sweet peace is shed—
But ah, the old pain that the waking brings,
That lives again so soon as sleep is fled.
    Man, why should thought of death cause you to weep,
    Since death is but an endless, dreamless sleep.

The Greatest of These Is War

Around the council-board of hell, with Satan at their
    head,
The three great scourges of humanity sat.
Gaunt Famine, with hollow cheek and voice, arose and
    spoke:
"O Prince, I have stalked the earth,
And my victims by ten thousands I have slain.
I have smitten old and young.
Mouths of the helpless old moaning for bread, I have
    filled with dust;
And I have laughed to see a crying babe tug at the
    shriveling breast
Of its mother, dead and cold.
I have heard the cries and prayers of men go up to a
    tearless sky,
And fall back upon an earth of ashes;
But, heedless, I have gone on with my work.
'Tis thus, O Prince, that I have scourged mankind."

And Satan nodded his head.

Pale Pestilence, with stenchful breath, then spoke and
    said:
"Great Prince, my brother, Famine, attacks the poor.
He is most terrible against the helpless and the old.
But I have made a charnel-house of the mightiest cities
    of men.

When I strike, neither their stores of gold or of grain
    avail.
With a breath I lay low their strongest, and wither up
    their fairest.
I come upon them without warning, lancing invisible
    death.
From me they flee with eyes and mouths distended;
I poison the air for which they gasp, and I strike them
    down fleeing.
'Tis thus, great Prince, that I have scourged mankind."

And Satan nodded his head.

Then the red monster, War, rose up and spoke;
His blood-shot eyes glared round him, and his
    thundering voice
Echoed through the murky vaults of hell:
"O, mighty Prince, my brothers, Famine and Pestilence,
Have slain their thousands and ten thousands—true;
But the greater their victories have been,
The more have they wakened in Man's breast
The God-like attributes of sympathy, of brotherhood
    and love
And made of him a searcher after wisdom.
But I arouse in Man the demon and the brute,
I plant black hatred in his heart and red revenge.
From the summit of fifty thousand years of upward
    climb
I haul him down to the level of the start, back to the wolf.
I give him claws.
I set his teeth into his brother's throat.

I make him drunk with his brother's blood.
And I laugh ho! ho! while he destroys himself.
O mighty Prince, not only do I slay,
I draw Man hellward."

And Satan smiled, stretched out his hand, and said:
"O War, of all the scourges of humanity, I crown you
    chief."

And hell rang with the acclamation of the Fiends.

A Poet to His Baby Son

Tiny bit of humanity,
Blessed with your mother's face,
And cursed with your father's mind.

I say cursed with your father's mind,
Because you can lie so long and so quietly on your back,
Playing with the dimpled big toe of your left foot,
And looking away,
Through the ceiling of the room, and beyond.
Can it be that already you are thinking of being a poet?

Why don't you kick and howl,
And make the neighbors talk about
"That damned baby next door,"
And make up your mind forthwith
To grow up and be a banker
Or a politician or some other sort of go-getter
Or—?—whatever you decide upon,
Rid yourself of these incipient thoughts
About being a poet.

For poets no longer are makers of songs,
Chanters of the gold and purple harvest,
Sayers of the glories of earth and sky,
Of the sweet pain of love
And the keen joy of living;
No longer dreamers of the essential dreams,

And interpreters of the eternal truth,
Through the eternal beauty.
Poets these days are unfortunate fellows.
Baffled in trying to say old things in a new way
Or new things in an old language,
They talk abracadabra
In an unknown tongue,
Each one fashioning for himself
A wordy world of shadow problems,
And as a self-imagined Atlas,
Struggling under it with puny legs and arms,
Groaning out incoherent complaints at his load.

My son, this is no time nor place for a poet;
Grow up and join the big, busy crowd
That scrambles for what it thinks it wants
Out of this old world which is—as it is—
And, probably, always will be.

Take the advice of a father who knows:
You cannot begin too young
Not to be a poet.

Dialect Poems

Twenty-five years ago traditional dialect was regarded as the natural mode of expression for Negro American poets. By a great many people it was considered the exclusive mode; and, no doubt, there are some people who still feel that way about it. Today no Negro American poet uses the traditional dialect as a medium. When he does use dialect it is the racy, living speech of the Negro in certain phases of contemporary life. Conventionalized dialect has been left entirely to white writers.

The passing of traditional dialect as a medium for Negro poets is complete. They realize that its essential *motif*—contented, childlike, happy-go-lucky, humorous, or forlorn "darkies" with their banjos, their singing and dancing, their watermelons and possums, painted in standardized colors against a background of log cabins, cotton fields, and lazy rivers—is itself a smooth-worn stereotype. Even the reader is conscious that almost all poetry in the conventionalized dialect is either based on the comic minstrel traditions of Negro life—traditions that were extremely exaggerated and that often had no relation at all to actual Negro life—or is permeated with excessive sentimentality. Both the poets and their readers now realize that as an instrument the old dialect has but two main stops, humor and pathos. The poets, at any rate, understand that this restricted gamut is too narrow for the interpretation or even the presentation of present-day Negro life.

This limitation is not inherent in the dialect as dialect; that is fully demonstrated in its use in the folk creations. The limitation is due to the artificial conventions that have been fixed upon the dialect as a literary medium by white influences, and the conformity to those conventions by the individual writers. And herein lies the distinction between the use of the dialect by the individual writers and by the folk creators; the former felt the pressure of an outside audience, while the latter worked solely to express and please themselves. If Negro American poets, writing only to express themselves and voice their race, had been the first to use and develop the dialect as a written form, if they had been the ones to work it in its virgin state, they would, without doubt, have created a medium of great flexibility and range, a medium comparable to what Burns made of the Scottish dialect.

The possibility of doing that, however, no longer exists. If the Negro poet today wishes to express himself in a larger way in folk speech, he must, as I stated in the preface to *The Book of American Negro Poetry*, do some such thing as Synge did for Irish speech; that is, he needs to find a form that will express the racial spirit by symbols from within rather than by symbols from without (such as the mere mutilation of English spelling and pronunciation). He needs a form that is larger and freer than conventionalized plantation dialect, but which will still hold the racial flavor; a form expressing the uninhibited imagery, the distinctive idioms and turns of thought, and, too, the distinctive humor and pathos of the Negro, but which will be capable of voicing the deepest and highest emotions and aspirations, of covering the widest scope of subjects and treatment, and of manifesting in full Negro life and spirit. I myself was attempting to find such a form in the writing of *God's Trombones*.

But taking the situation as it is—Negro folk speech being a form native only to a minority group, and in that respect quite unlike Scottish folk speech—the Negro poet in the United States finds that for achieving the most comprehensive and most comprehensible expression his medium must be American speech.

Yet, notwithstanding all I have so far said, much has been done in the traditional dialect with more tenderness and charm, with a gentler humor, a keener poignancy, and a wider appeal than, probably, would have been possible through any other medium. To take Dunbar's dialect poetry out of American literature would cause both a racial and a national loss.

The several dialect verses which follow, and which I was, at first, reluctant to include, are early poems and belong to the traditional type. They have been selected from the section, "Jingles and Croons," in *Fifty Years and Other Poems*.

Ma Lady's Lips Am Like de Honey

(NEGRO LOVE SONG)

Breeze a-sighin', and a-blowin',
Southern summer night.
Stars a-gleamin' and a-glowin',
Moon jes shinin' right.
Strollin', like all lovers do,
Down de lane wid Lindy Lou;
Honey on her lips to waste;
'Speck I'm gwine to steal a taste.

   Oh, ma lady's lips am like de honey,
   Ma lady's lips am like de rose;
   An' I'm jes like de little bee a-buzzin'
   'Round de flower wha' de nectah grows.
   Ma lady's lips dey smile so temptin',
   Ma lady's teeth so w'ite dey shine,
   Oh, ma lady's lips so tantalizin',
   Ma lady's lips so close to mine.

Bird a-whistlin' and a-swayin'
In de live-oak tree;
Seems to me he keeps a-sayin',
"Kiss dat gal fo' me!"
Look heah, Mister Mockin' Bird,
Gwine to take you at yo' word;
If I meets ma Waterloo,
Gwine to blame it all on you.

Honey in de rose, I s'pose, is
Put der fo' de bee;
Honey on her lips, I knows, is
Put der jes fo' me.
Seen a sparkle in her eye,
Heard her heave a little sigh;
Felt her kinder squeeze ma han',
'Nuff to make me understan'.

Oh, ma lady's lips am like de honey,
Ma lady's lips am like de rose;
An' I'm jes like de little bee a-buzzin'
'Round de flower wha' de nectah grows.
Ma lady's lips dey smile so temptin',
Ma lady's teeth so w'ite dey shine,
Oh, ma lady's lips so tantalizin',
Ma lady's lips so close to mine.

A Plantation Bacchanal

W'en ole Mister Sun gits tiah'd a-hangin'
High up in de sky;
W'en de rain am a-fallin' an' de thunder am a-bangin',
An' de crap's done all laid by;
W'en yo' bones growin' chilly wid de rheumatics,
Den yo' ride de mule to town,
Git a great big jug o' de ole corn juice,
An' w'en you drink her down—

    Jes lay away ole Trouble,
    An' dry up all yo' tears;
    Yo' pleasure sho' to double
    An' you bound to lose yo' keers.
    Jes lay away ole Sorrer
    High up on de shelf;
    And never mind tomorrer,
    'Twill take care of itself.

W'en ole Mister Age begins a-stealin'
Thoo yo' back an' knees,
W'en yo' bones an' jints lose der limber feelin',
An' am stiff'nin' by degrees;
Now der's jes one way to feel young and spry
W'en you heah dem banjos soun';
Git a great big swig o' de ole corn juice,
An' w'en you drink her down—

Jes lay away ole Trouble,
An' dry up all yo' tears;
Yo' pleasure sho' to double
An' you bound to lose yo' keers.
Jes lay away ole Sorrer
High up on de shelf;
And never mind tomorrer,
'Twill take care of itself.

Tunk

Look heah, Tunk!—Now, ain't dis awful! T'ought I sont
    you off to school.
Don't you know dat you is growin' up to be a reg'lah
    fool?

Whah's dem books dat I's done bought you? Look heah,
    boy, you tell me quick,
Whah's dat Webster blue-back spellah an' dat bran' new
    'rifmatic?

W'ile I'm t'inkin' you is lahnin' in de school, why bless
    ma soul!
You off in de woods a-playin'. Can't you do like you is
    tole?

Boy, I tell you, it's jes scan'lous d'way dat you is goin' on.
An' you sholy go'n be sorry, jes as true as you is bo'n.

Heah I'm tryin' hard to raise you as a credit to dis race,
An' you tryin' heap much harder fu' to come up in
    disgrace.

Dese de days w'en men don't git up to de top by hooks
    an' crooks;
Tell you now, dey's got to git der standin' on a pile o'
    books.

W'en you sees a black man goin' to de fiel' as soon as light,
Follerin' a mule across it f'om de mawnin' tel de night,

Wukin' all his life fu' vittles, hoein' 'tween de cott'n
rows,
W'en he knocks off ole an' tiah'd, wid nut'n but his
ragged clo'es,

You kin put it down to ignunce, aftah all what's done an'
said,
You kin bet dat dat same black man ain't got nut'n in his
head.

Ain't you seed dem w'ite men set'n in der awfice? Don't
you know
Dey goes der 'bout nine each mawnin'—bless yo' soul,
dey's out by fo'.

Dey jes does a little writin'; does dat by some easy means;
Gals jes set an' play piannah on dem print'n press
muchines.

Chile, dem men knows how to figgah, how to use dat
little pen,
An' dey knows dat blue-back spellah f'om beginnin' to
de en'.

Dat's de 'fect of education; dat's de t'ing what's gwine to
rule;
Git dem books, you lazy rascal! Git back to yo' place in
school.

Brer Rabbit, You's de Cutes' of 'Em All

Once der was a meetin' in de wilderness,
All de critters of creation dey was dar;
Brer Rabbit, Brer Possum, Brer Wolf, Brer Fox,
King Lion, Mister Terrapin, Mister B'ar.
De question fu' discussion was, "Who is de bigges' man?"
Dey 'pinted ole Jedge Owl to decide;
He polished up his spectacles an' put 'em on his nose,
An' to the question slowly he replied:

"Brer Wolf am mighty cunnin',
Brer Fox am mighty sly,
Brer Terrapin and Possum—kinder small;
Brer Lion's mighty vicious,
Brer B'ar he's sorter 'spicious,
Brer Rabbit, you's de cutes' of 'em all."

Dis caused a great confusion 'mongst de animals,
Ev'y critter claimed dat he had won de prize;
Dey 'sputed an' dey arg'ed, dey growled an' dey roared,
Den putty soon de dus' begin to rise.
Brer Rabbit he jes' stood aside an' watched 'em w'ile dey
    fight,
Brer Lion he mos' tore Brer B'ar in two;
W'en dey was all so tiah'd dat dey couldn't catch der bref
Brer Rabbit he jes' grabbed de prize an' flew.

Brer Wolf am mighty cunnin',
Brer Fox am mighty sly,
Brer Terrapin an' Possum—kinder small;
Brer Lion's mighty vicious,
Brer B'ar he's sorter 'spicious,
Brer Rabbit, you's de cutes' of 'em all.

Answer to Prayer

Der ain't no use in sayin' de Lawd won't answer prah;
If you knows how to ax Him, I knows He's bound to
heah.

De trouble is, some people don't ax de proper way,
Den w'en dey git's no answer dey doubts de use to pray.

You got to use egzac'ly de 'spressions an' de words
To show dat 'tween yo' faith an' works, you 'pends on
works two-thirds.

Now, one time I remember—jes how long I won't say—
I thought I'd like a turkey to eat on Chris'mus day

Fu' weeks I dreamed 'bout turkeys, a-strutt'n in der
pride;
But seed no way to git one—widout de Lawd pervide.

An' so I went to prayin', I pray'd wid all my might:
"Lawd, sen' *to* me a turkey." I pray'd bofe day an' night.

"Lawd sen' *to* me a turkey, a big one if you please."
I 'clar to heaben I pray'd so much I mos' wore out ma
knees.

I pray'd dat prah so often, I pray'd dat prah so long,
Yet didn't git no turkey, I knowed 'twas sump'n wrong.

So on de night 'fore Chris'mus w'en I got down to pray,
"Lawd, sen' *me* to a turkey," I had de sense to say.

"Lawd sen' *me* to a turkey." I know dat prah was right,
An' it was sholy answer'd; I got de bird dat night.

A Banjo Song

W'en de banjos wuz a-ringin',
'N' evehbody wuz a-singin',
Oh, wuzen dem de good times sho!
All de ole folks would be chattin',
An' de pickaninnies pattin',
As dey heah'd de feet a-shufflin' 'cross de flo'.

An' how we'd dance, an' how we'd sing!
Dance tel de day done break.
An' how dem banjos dey would ring,
An' de cabin flo' would shake!

Come along, come along,
Come along, come along,
Don't you heah dem banjos a-ringin'?

Gib a song, gib a song,
Gib a song, gib a song,
Git yo' feet fixed up fu' a-wingin'.

W'ile de banjos dey go plunka-plunka-plunk,
We'll dance tel de ole flo' shake;
W'ile de feet keep a-goin' chooka-chooka-chook,
We'll dance tel de day done break.

The Rivals

Look heah! Is I evah tole you 'bout de curious way I won
Anna Liza? Say, I nevah? Well heah's how de thing wuz
    done.

Lize, you know, wuz mighty purty—dat's been forty
    yeahs ago—
'N' 'cos to look at her dis minit, you might'n s'pose dat
    it wuz so.

She wuz jes de greates' 'traction in de country, 'n' bless
    de Lam'!
Eveh lovin' man wuz co'tin', but it lay 'twix me an' Sam.

You know Sam. We both wuz wu'kin' on de ole John
    Tompkin's place.
'N' evehbody wuz a-watchin' t'see who's gwine to win
    de race.

Hee! hee! hee! Now you mus' raley 'scuse me fu' dis
    snickering,
But I jes can't he'p f'om laffin' eveh time I tells dis thing.

Ez I wuz a-sayin', me an' Sam wu'ked daily side by side,
He a-studyin', me a-studyin' how to win Lize fu' a bride.

Well, de race wuz kinder equal, Lize wuz sorter on de
    fence;
Sam he had de mostes dollars, an' I had de mostes sense.

Things dey run along 'bout eben tel der come Big
Meetin' day;
Sam den thought, to win Miss Liza, he had foun' de
shoest way.

An' you talk about big meetin's! None been like it 'fore
nor sence;
Der wuz sich a crowd o' people dat we had to put up
tents.

Der wuz preachers f'om de Eas', an' der wuz preachers
f'om de Wes';
Folks had kilt mos' eveh chicken, an wuz fattenin' up
de res'.

Gals had all got new w'ite dresses, an' bought ribbens
fu' der hair,
Fixin' fu' de openin' Sunday, prayin' dat de day'd be
fair.

Dat de Reveren' Jasper Jones of Mount Moriah, it wuz
'llowed,
Wuz to preach de openin' sermon; so you know der
wuz a crowd.

Fu' dat man wuz sho' a preacher; had a voice jes like a
bull;
So der ain't no use in sayin' dat de meetin' house wuz full.

Folks wuz der f'om Big Pine Hollow, some come 'way
    f'om Muddy Creek,
Some come jes to stay fu' Sunday, but de crowd stay'd
    thoo de week.

Some come ridin' in top-buggies wid de w'eels all painted
    red,
Pulled by mules dat run like rabbits, each one tryin' to
    git ahead.

Othah po'rer folks come drivin' mules dat leaned up
    'ginst de shaf',
Hitched to broke-down, creaky wagons dat looked like
    dey'd drap in half.

But de bigges' crowd come walkin', wid der new shoes
    on der backs;
'Scuse wuz dat dey couldn't weah em 'cause de heels
    wuz full o' tacks.

Fact is, it's a job for Job, a-trudgin' in de sun an' heat,
Down a long an' dusty clay road wid yo' shoes packed
    full o' feet.

'Cose dey stopt an' put dem shoes on w'en dey got mos'
    to de do';
Den dey had to grin an' bear it; dat tuk good religion
    sho.

But I mos' forgot ma story—well at las' dat Sunday came
And it seemed dat evehbody, blin' an' deef, an' halt an'
    lame

Wuz out in de grove a-waitin' fu' de meetin' to begin;
Ef dat crowd had got converted 'twould a been de end
    o' sin.

Lize wuz der in all her glory, purty ez a big sunflowah.
I kin 'member how she looked jes same ez 'twuz dis ve'y
    houah.

But to make my story shorter, w'ile we wuz a-waitin'
    der,
Down de road we spied a cloud o' dus' dat filled up all
    de air.

An' ez we kep' on a-lookin', out f'om 'mongst dat ve'y
    cloud,
Sam, on Marse John's big mule, Cæsar, rode right slam
    up in de crowd.

You jes oughtah seed dat feller, 'clar I like tah los' ma
    bref;
Fu' to use a common 'spression, he wuz 'bout nigh
    dressed to def.

He had slipped to town dat Sat'day, didn't let nobody
    know,

An' had carried all his cash an' lef' it in de dry-goods
    sto'.

He had on a bran' new suit o' sto'-bought clo'es, a high
    plug hat;
He looked 'zactly like a gen'man, 'tain't no use d'nyin'
    dat.

W'en he got down off dat mule an' bowed to Liza I
    could see
How she looked at him so 'dmirin', an' jes kinder glanced
    at me.

Den I know'd to win dat gal, I sho' would need some
    othah means
'Sides a-hangin' 'round big meetin' in a suit o' homespun
    jeans.

W'en dey blowed de ho'n fu' preachin', an' de crowd all
    went inside,
I jes felt ez doh I'd like tah go off in de woods an' hide.

So I stay'd outside de meetin', set'n underneat' de trees,
Seemed to me I sot der ages, wid ma elbows on ma knees.

W'en dey sung dat hymn, "Nobody knows de trouble
    dat I see,"
Seem'd to me dat dey wuz singin' eveh word o' it fu' me.

Jes how long I might ha' sot der, actin' like a cussed fool,

I don't know, but it jes happen'd dat I look'd an' saw
 Sam's mule,

An' de thought come slowly tricklin' thoo ma brain
 right der an' den,
Dat, perhaps, wid some persuasion, I could make dat
 mule ma fren'.

An' I jes kep' on a-thinkin', an' I kep' a-lookin' 'roun',
Tel I spied two great big san' spurs right close by me on
 de groun'.

Well, I took dem spurs an' put em underneat' o' Cæsar's
 saddle,
So dey'd press down in his backbone soon ez Sam had
 got a-straddle.

'Twuz a pretty ticklish job, an' jes ez soon ez it wuz
 done,
I went back w'ere I wuz set'n fu' to wait an' see de fun.

Purty soon heah come de people, jes a-swa'min' out
 de do',
Talkin' 'bout de "pow'ful sermon"—"nevah heah'd de
 likes befo'."

How de "monahs fell convicted" jes de same ez lumps
 o' lead,
How dat some wuz still a-layin' same ez if dey'd been
 struck dead.

An' to rectly heah come Liza, Sam a-strollin' by her side,
An' it seem'd to me his smile wuz jest about twelve inches
    wide.

Look to me like he had swelled up to 'bout twice his
    natchul size,
An' I heah'd him say, "I'd like to be yo' 'scort tonight,
    Miss Lize."

Den he made a bow jes like he's gwine to make a speech
    in school,
An' walk'd off ez proud ez Marse John, over to ontie
    his mule,

W'en Sam's foot fust touched de stirrup he know'd der
    wuz sump'n wrong;
'Cuz de mule begin to tremble an' to sorter side along.

W'en Sam raised his weight to mount him, Cæsar
    bristled up his ear,
W'en Sam sot down in de saddle, den dat mule
    commenced to rear.

An' he reared an' pitched an' caper'd, only ez a mule kin
    pitch,
Tel he flung Sam clean f'om off him, landed him squar'
    in a ditch.

W'en Sam riz up, well, I tell you, I felt kinder bad fu'
    him;

He had bust dem cheap sto' britches f'om de center to
    de rim.

All de plug hat dat wuz lef' him wuz de brim aroun' his
    neck,
Smear'd wid mud f'om top to bottom—well, he wuz a
    sight, I 'speck.

Wuz de folks a-laffin'? Well su', I jes sholy thought dey'd
    bus'.
Wuz Sam laffin'? 'Twuz de fus' time dat I evah heah'd
    him cuss.

W'ile Sam slink'd off thoo de back woods I walk'd
    slowly home wid Lize.
W'en I axed her jes one question der wuz sump'n in her
    eyes

Made me know der wuz no need o' any answer bein'
    said,
An' I felt jes like de whole world wuz a-spinnin' roun'
    ma head.

So I said, "Lize, w'en we marry, mus' I weah some
    sto'-bought clo'es?"
She says, "Jeans is good enough fu' any po' folks, heaben
    knows!"

Sence You Went Away

Seems lak to me de stars don't shine so bright,
Seems lak to me de sun done loss his light,
Seems lak to me der's nothin' goin' right,
  Sence you went away.

Seems lak to me de sky ain't half so blue,
Seems lak to me dat ev'ything wants you,
Seems lak to me I don't know what to do,
  Sence you went away.

Seems lak to me dat ev'ything is wrong,
Seems lak to me de day's jes twice ez long,
Seems lak to me de bird's forgot his song,
  Sence you went away.

Seems lak to me I jes can't he'p but sigh,
Seems lak to me ma th'oat keeps gittin' dry,
Seems lak to me a tear stays in ma eye,
  Sence you went away.

Fifty Years

I had for some while been revolving in my mind the idea of writing a poem in commemoration of the fiftieth anniversary of the signing of the Emancipation Proclamation. Because of some mental quirk I kept thinking that that anniversary would fall in 1915. In the early part of October, 1912, I learned that the fiftieth anniversary of the preliminary proclamation, which Lincoln signed September 22, 1862, was being celebrated; and I realized that I had, instead of a little more than two years, only a little more than two months in which to do the poem. I was at the time on consular duty in Nicaragua, and in the midst of the beginning of the American military occupation of that country. The consulate had been made Marine headquarters, there was constant coming and going of officers and troops; machine-guns were mounted in front of the house, and at night a hundred or more Marines slept in the *patio*. I found it possible to write only after midnight.

I finished the poem in the first part of December and sent it to my friend, Brander Matthews, at Columbia University. Professor Matthews sent it to the *New York Times*, and it was published in that newspaper on January 1, 1913, the precise date of the fiftieth anniversary.

As first written, the poem consisted of forty-one stanzas. At the point where it reached its highest expression of achievement and of faith in the realization of well-earned rights, it took a turn and brought into view the other side of the shield, and ended on a note of bitterness and despair. I saw that the last part of the composition, though voicing the verities, nullified the theme, purpose, and effect of the poem as a whole. After a struggle in which my better taste and judgment won, I cut off the last stanzas.

Fifty Years

(1863–1913)

O brothers mine, today we stand
    Where half a century sweeps our ken,
Since God, through Lincoln's ready hand,
    Struck off our bonds and made us men.

Just fifty years—a winter's day,
    As runs the history of a race;
Yet, as we look back o'er the way,
    How distant seems our starting place!

Look farther back! Three centuries!
    To where a naked, shivering score,
Snatched from their haunts across the seas,
    Stood, wide-eyed, on Virginia's shore.

Then let us here erect a stone,
    To mark the place, to mark the time;
As witness to God's purpose shown,
    A pledge to hold this day sublime.

A part of His unknown design,
    We've lived within a mighty age;
And we have helped to write a line
    On history's most wondrous page.

A few black bondmen strewn along
    The borders of our eastern coast,
Now grown a race, ten million strong,
    An upward, onward, marching host.

Far, far the way that we have trod,
    From slave and pagan denizens,
To freedmen, freemen, sons of God,
    Americans and Citizens.

For never let the thought arise
    That we are here on sufferance bare;
Outcasts asylumed 'neath these skies,
    And aliens without part or share.

This land is ours by right of birth,
    This land is ours by right of toil;
We helped to turn its virgin earth,
    Our sweat is in its fruitful soil.

Where once the tangled forest stood,
    Where flourished once rank weed and thorn,
Behold the path-traced, peaceful wood,
    The cotton white, the yellow corn.

To gain these fruits that have been earned,
    To hold these fields that have been won,
Our arms have strained, our backs have burned,
    Bent bare beneath a ruthless sun.

That Banner which is now the type
    Of victory on field and flood—
Remember, its first crimson stripe
    Was dyed by Attucks' willing blood.

And never yet has come the cry—
    When that fair flag has been assailed—
For men to do, for men to die,
    That we have faltered or have failed.

We've helped to bear it, rent and torn,
    Through many a hot-breath'd battle breeze;
Held in our hands, it has been borne
    And planted far across the seas.

And never yet—O haughty Land,
    Let us, at least, for this be praised—
Has one black, treason-guided hand
    Ever against that flag been raised.

Then should we speak but servile words,
    Or shall we hang our heads in shame?
Stand back of new-come foreign hordes,
    And fear our heritage to claim?

No! Stand erect and without fear,
    And for our foes let this suffice—
We've brought a rightful sonship here,
    And we have more than paid the price.

And yet, my brothers, well I know
  The tethered feet, the pinioned wings,
The spirit bowed beneath the blow,
  The heart grown faint from wounds and stings;

The staggering force of brutish might,
  That strikes and leaves us stunned and dazed;
The long, vain waiting through the night
  To hear some voice for justice raised.

Full well I know the hour when hope
  Sinks dead, and round us everywhere
Hangs stifling darkness, and we grope
  With hands uplifted in despair.

Courage! Look out, beyond, and see
  The far horizon's beckoning span!
Faith in your God-known destiny!
  We are a part of some great plan.

Because the tongues of Garrison
  And Phillips now are cold in death,
Think you their work can be undone?
  Or quenched the fires lit by their breath?

Think you that John Brown's spirit stops?
  That Lovejoy was but idly slain?
Or do you think those precious drops
  From Lincoln's heart were shed in vain?

That for which millions prayed and sighed,
    That for which tens of thousands fought,
For which so many freely died,
    God cannot let it come to naught.

Lift Every Voice and Sing

A group of young men in Jacksonville, Florida, arranged to celebrate Lincoln's birthday in 1900. My brother, J. Rosamond Johnson, and I decided to write a song to be sung at the exercises. I wrote the words and he wrote the music. Our New York publisher, Edward B. Marks, made mimeographed copies for us, and the song was taught to and sung by a chorus of five hundred colored school children.

Shortly afterwards my brother and I moved away from Jacksonville to New York, and the song passed out of our minds. But the school children of Jacksonville kept singing it; they went off to other schools and sang it; they became teachers and taught it to other children. Within twenty years it was being sung over the South and in some other parts of the country. Today the song, popularly known as the Negro National Hymn, is quite generally used.

The lines of this song repay me in an elation, almost of exquisite anguish, whenever I hear them sung by Negro children.

Lift Every Voice and Sing

Lift every voice and sing
Till earth and heaven ring,
Ring with the harmonies of Liberty;
Let our rejoicing rise
High as the listening skies,
Let it resound loud as the rolling sea.
Sing a song full of the faith that the dark past has
    taught us,
Sing a song full of the hope that the present has
    brought us.
Facing the rising sun of our new day begun,
Let us march on till victory is won.

Stony the road we trod,
Bitter the chastening rod,
Felt in the days when hope unborn had died;
Yet with a steady beat,
Have not our weary feet
Come to the place for which our fathers sighed?
We have come over a way that with tears has been
    watered,
We have come, treading our path through the blood of
    the slaughtered,
Out from the gloomy past,
Till now we stand at last
Where the white gleam of our bright star is cast.

God of our weary years,
God of our silent tears,
Thou who hast brought us thus far on the way;
Thou who hast by Thy might
Led us into the light,
Keep us forever in the path, we pray.
Lest our feet stray from the places, our God, where we
        met Thee,
Lest, our hearts drunk with the wine of the world, we
    forget Thee;
Shadowed beneath Thy hand,
May we forever stand.
True to our God,
True to our native land.

Envoy

If homely virtues draw from me a tune
In jingling rhyme—or in ambitious rune;
Or if the smoldering future should inspire
My hand to try the seer's prophetic lyre;
Or if injustice, brutishness, and wrong
Stir me to make a weapon of my song;

O God, give beauty, truth, strength to my words—
Oh, may they fall like sweetly cadenced chords,
Or burn like beacon fires from out the dark,
Or speed like arrows, swift and sure to the mark.

A Note on Plácido's "Mother, Farewell!"

Plácido, in some respects the greatest of all the Cuban poets, was born in Havana in 1809. It is safe to say that no native poet is better known or better loved by the Cuban people. His birth, his life, and his death ideally contained the tragic elements that go into the making of a halo about a poet's head. His early life was a struggle against poverty; his youth and manhood a struggle for Cuban independence. His death placed him in the list of Cuban martyrs; on June 27, 1844, he was lined up against a wall with ten others and shot by order of the Spanish authorities on the charge of conspiracy. In his short but eventful life he turned out work that bulked more than six hundred pages. During the last few hours preceding his execution he wrote three of his best-known poems, among them his famous sonnet, "Mother, Farewell!"

This sonnet has been translated into every important language; but, in spite of its wide popularity, it is, outside of Cuba, the least understood of all of Plácido's poems. The key to the poem is the first word, and the first word in the Spanish is *si* (if).

While Plácido's father was a Negro, his mother was a Spanish white woman. At his birth she abandoned him to a foundling hospital, and perhaps never saw him again, although it is known that she outlived her son. When the poet came down to his last hours he remembered that somewhere there was a woman who was his mother—that although she had heartlessly abandoned him, that although he owed her no filial duty, still she might, perhaps, on hearing of his tragic end, feel some pang of grief or regret; so he tells her in his last words that he dies happy and bids her not to weep. This he does with nobility and dignity, but absolutely without affection. Taking into account these facts and their humiliating and embittering effect upon a soul so sensitive as Plácido's, this sonnet is a remarkably fine piece of work. For these reasons I have chosen for inclusion here my translation of this poem above others that I have made from Plácido.

FOR THE BEST IN PAPERBACKS, LOOK FOR THE Ⓟ

In every corner of the world, on every subject under the sun, Penguin represents quality and variety—the very best in publishing today.

For complete information about books available from Penguin—including Puffins, Penguin Classics, and Arkana—and how to order them, write to us at the appropriate address below. Please note that for copyright reasons the selection of books varies from country to country.

In the United Kingdom: Please write to *Dept. EP, Penguin Books Ltd, Bath Road, Harmondsworth, West Drayton, Middlesex UB7 0DA.*

In the United States: Please write to *Penguin Putnam Inc., P.O. Box 12289 Dept. B, Newark, New Jersey 07101-5289* or call 1-800-788-6262.

In Canada: Please write to *Penguin Books Canada Ltd, 10 Alcorn Avenue, Suite 300, Toronto, Ontario M4V 3B2.*

In Australia: Please write to *Penguin Books Australia Ltd, P.O. Box 257, Ringwood, Victoria 3134.*

In New Zealand: Please write to *Penguin Books (NZ) Ltd, Private Bag 102902, North Shore Mail Centre, Auckland 10.*

In India: Please write to *Penguin Books India Pvt Ltd, 11 Panchsheel Shopping Centre, Panchsheel Park, New Delhi 110 017.*

In the Netherlands: Please write to *Penguin Books Netherlands bv, Postbus 3507, NL-1001 AH Amsterdam.*

In Germany: Please write to *Penguin Books Deutschland GmbH, Metzlerstrasse 26, 60594 Frankfurt am Main.*

In Spain: Please write to *Penguin Books S. A., Bravo Murillo 19, 1° B, 28015 Madrid.*

In Italy: Please write to *Penguin Italia s.r.l., Via Benedetto Croce 2, 20094 Corsico, Milano.*

In France: Please write to *Penguin France, Le Carré Wilson, 62 rue Benjamin Baillaud, 31500 Toulouse.*

In Japan: Please write to *Penguin Books Japan Ltd, Kaneko Building, 2-3-25 Koraku, Bunkyo-Ku, Tokyo 112.*

In South Africa: Please write to *Penguin Books South Africa (Pty) Ltd, Private Bag X14, Parkview, 2122 Johannesburg.*

BAKER & TAYLOR